bucket list
Book for Couples

Copyright 2021 by Nancy Moore

Table of contents

1 getting started

10 important life questions for each partner to ask themselves.

What am I good at?

For HIM

For HER

What am I so-so at?

For HIM

For HER

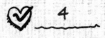

What am I bad at?

For HIM

For HER

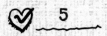

What makes me tired?

For HIM

For HER

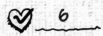 6

What is the most important thing in my life?

For HIM

For HER

Who are the most important people in my life?

For HIM

_____
_____
_____
_____
_____
_____
_____
_____

For HER

_____
_____
_____
_____
_____
_____
_____
_____

How much sleep do I need?

For HIM

For HER

9

What stresses me out?

For HIM

For HER

What relaxes me?

For HIM

For HER

What's my definition of success?

For HIM

For HER

----

2 about us

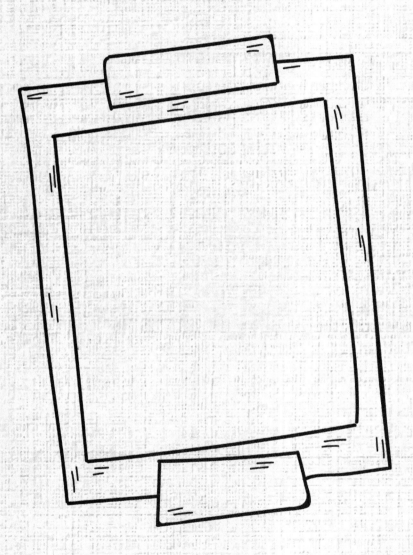

who we are ?

For HIM

1. My name is_____.
2. I am _____ years old.
3. I am from _____.
4. I live in_____.
5. My telephone number is_____.
6. My address is_____.
7. I am a/an_____.
8. My favorite sport is_____.
9. My favorite animal is the_____.
10. My birthday is on_____.
11. My favorite color is_____.
12. I have_____ brother(s) and _____ sister(s)/I'm an only child.

For HER

1. My name is_____.
2. I am _____ years old.
3. I am from _____.
4. I live in_____.
5. My telephone number is_____.
6. My address is_____.
7. I am a/an_____.
8. My favorite sport is_____.
9. My favorite animal is the_____.
10. My birthday is on_____.
11. My favorite color is_____.
12. I have_____ brother(s) and _____ sister(s)/I'm an only child.

who we want to be?

For HIM

For HER

----

what we like ?

For HIM

For HER

16

our hobbies ?

For HIM

For HER

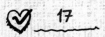

what we do in free time ?

For HIM

For HER

----

favorite food ?

For HIM

For HER

write together

what one of us like that other one can't stand?

it's a very important part because each partner wants to have a great time during their adventure. Last thing that a couple wants during the journey is quarrel.

----

what makes you happy?

----

what is an ideal weekend for you?

----

where you always wanted to travel ?

-- --------------------------------------
--- --------------------------------------

----

what we like about sex ?

-- --------------------------------------

----

what things we would like to do before we die?

List for 10 most important things

1 _____

2 _____

3 _____

4 _____

5 _____

6 _____

7 _____

8 _____

9 _____

10 _____

3 bucket list ideas

150 Bucket List Ideas for Couple

1. Swim in each of the four major oceans
2. Visit at least three out of the seven new Wonders of the World
3. Touch six out of the seven continents (Antarctica is optional!)
4. Helicopter ride over the Grand Canyon
5. Road trip across the entire United States
6. Go on a week-long cruise
7. Experience the Northern Lights
8. Dive at the Great Barrier Reef
9. Hike through the Himalayas
10. Go on a wildlife safari
11. Kiss on Top of a London Eye
12. Create a Music Playlist of Your Relationship
13. Learn to Tango
14. Attend the Concert of a Band You Both Love
15. Make each other t-shirts.
16. Volunteer together.
17. Go to Disneyland.
18. Have a sex marathon for a day.
19. Ride a rollercoaster together.
20. Sing in public together.
21. Kiss underwater.
22. Attend an Opera.

23. Take a photo together each day for a year.

24. Kiss at midnight on December 31st.

25. Play a sexy game of twister.

26. Soak in a hot spring.

27. Island hop around Greece

28. Spend a week camping off the grid

29. Spend a week in each of the major "global" cities
    (New York, Paris, London, and Tokyo)

30. Swim with wild pigs in Exuma, Bahamas

31. Get VIP passes to a show/concert

32. Go Bowling

33. Master a new work-related skill each year

34. Create your own sex board or card game.

35. Establish a healthy work-life balance

36. Go to the theater

37. Have a car sex

38. Have a positive work attitude every day

39. Dress up in a couples costume for halloween

40. Have a marshmallow fight.

41. Name a star.

42. Make food and pass it out to the homeless.

43. Charter a yacht.

44. Become financially independent.

45. Tell someone how they've inspired you

46. Write poetry for each other.

47. Take a local factory tour.

48. Build your dream house out of Legos.

49. Support a cause that's important to you through donations or volunteering.

50. Retire early!

51. Take a Bubble Bath.

52. Go to a museum together.

53. Take more risks and try out-of-the-box ideas.

54. Have a party in Ibiza.

55. See an Amazing Cave.

56. Go fishing.

57. Get married.

58. Ride camels across a desert.

59. Go on Backpacking Trip Together.

60. Cycle Past Ancient Ruins.

61. Go vegetarian for one month.

62. Go vegan for one month.

63. Eat an entirely plant-based diet for one month!

64. Sing each other to sleep.

65. Meditate for 15 minutes every night before bed.

66. Participate in an archaeological dig.

67. Get a gym membership together.

68. Gamble in Vegas.

69. Dine out at a Fancy Restaurant.

70. Revisit the spot where you first kissed.

71. Host a couple's game night or family game night.

72. Stretch for five minutes every morning

73. Stand up and stretch every hour at work

74. Eliminate processed foods from your diet

75. Ride around town on a motorcycle.

76. Dance on the beach at sunset.

77. Spend a day at a spa and have a couple's massage

78. Escape from an escape room

79. Hug a koala

80. Try a new type of exercise such as cycling, weight lifting, or barre classes

81. Slow dance when there's no music playing.

82. Ride a gondola in Venice, Italy

83. Find something to laugh at every day

84. Take time to appreciate nature

85. RV across a country.

86. Organize your home and workspace — an organized life leads to an organized mind!

87. Try yoga, reiki, acupuncture, or another type of relaxing therapy

88. Spend time with people who make you happy

89. Hug a redwood.

90. Watch the Northern Lights in Iceland

91. Read five books about healthy finances

92. Visit an epic waterfall

93. Go rock climbing together.

94. Build up an emergency or rainy day fund

95. Start a family vacation fund

96. Catch Japan's cherry blossoms in full bloom

97. Spend the night at the ice hotel in Quebec

98. Attend a festival in Brazil

99. Learn ballroom or salsa dancing together

100. Buy your own home and pay off the mortgage

101. Donate regularly to a charity you're passionate about

102. Have a romantic photo session.

103. See the sunrise from the top of a mountain

104. Spend a night at a castle in Scotland

105. Get tattoos together.

106. Fully fund a charitable event

107. Have a baby.

108. Design your own house and build it.

109. Go to the Olympics or World Cup.

110. Become millionaires!

111. Teach your children the value of money from an early age

112. Start a spare change jar at home

113. Take out a life insurance policy

114. Take corny pictures in matching sweaters for your holiday cards.

115. Try to achieve a "no spend" month where you don't

buy anything extra outside regular bills

116. Donate to a charity of your children's choice
117. Keep accurate spending records
118. Create a family budgeting plan
119. Go green and save money on water and electricity bills
120. Go to a masquerade ball.
121. Become fluent in a new language
122. Play paintball.
123. Rent a beach house for the whole summer.
124. Take up knitting or crocheting
125. Try an extreme sport
126. Learn how to play an instrument
127. Kiss in the rain
128. Wake up to see the sunrise every day for a week
129. Adopt a rescue animal
130. Swim under a waterfall
131. Ride horses on the beach
132. Go bungee jumping
133. Take a hot air balloon ride
134. Visit an elephant sanctuary
135. Explore or spend a night in a real castle.
136. Draw each other.
137. Be in a parade float

138. Ride a mechanical bull

139. Go skinny dipping at night

140. Write a love letter

141. Drink champagne on the Eiffel Tower

142. Learn to play chess

143. Run a marathon, half marathon, or 5k

144. Conquer a lifelong fear

145. Learn how to cook an extravagant dish

146. Climb a glacier.

147. Paint a piece of art for your home

148. Learn how to drive a stick shift

149. Take a two-week vacation

150. Set a Guinness world record!

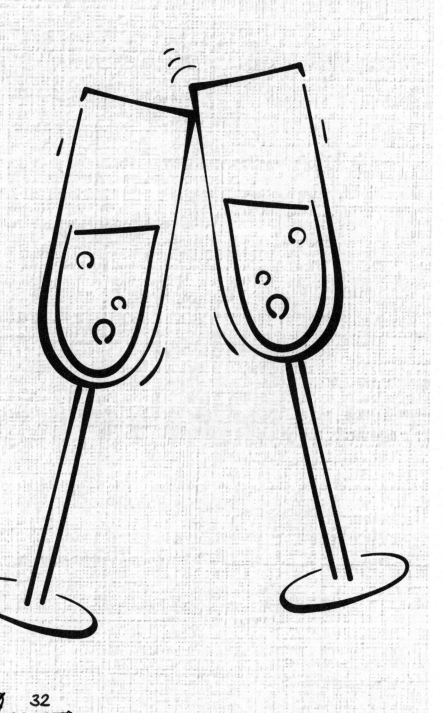

32

⟦4⟧ date bucket list

After completing the task mark the heart checkbox
Like This > ♥

ATTEND A *wine* TASTING ♡

DANCE TIL DAWN ♡

GO APPLE PICKING OR BERRY ♡
PICKING

BAKE TOGETHER ♡

HAVE A COUPLES BOOK CLUB, AND READ ♡
A BOOK AT THE SAME TIME

BUILD A BLANKET FORT ♡

 33

GO ON A ROMANTIC PICNIC ♡

GO SKINNY DIPPING ♡

jump in a pile of fresh fall leaves together ♡

RIDE IN A HOT AIR BALLOON♡

PADDLE A ROWBOAT AROUND A LAKE ♡

HOUSE SIT FOR FRIENDS (OR WHILE ♡ YOU TRAVEL!)

STAY AT A QUAINT BED & BREAKFAST-EVEN ♡
IF IT'S IN YOUR OWN TOWN

GET A COUPLES MASSAGE ♡

GO TO A COUNTY FAIR ♡

HOST A COUPLES GAME NIGHT ♡

EAT DINNER ON A BALCONY WITH
A STUNNING VIEW ♡

go to a museum and discuss
the exhibits ♡

 35

VOLUNTEER TOGETHER ♡

GO ICE SKATING ♡

WATCH EACH OTHER'S
FAVORITE MOVIE ♡

BINGE WATCH A TV SHOW TOGETHER ♡

MAKE DINNER FOR EACH OTHER ♡

 GET BUSY OUTSIDE ♡

HAVE A STAY-IN-BED-ALL-DAY
WEEKEND ♡

GET "SNOWED-IN" IN A COZY CABIN ♡

SLEEP UNDER THE STARS ☺ OR
BETTER YET, THE NORTHERN
LIGHTS ♡

SWIM WITH WHALE SHARKS - OR
OTHER INCREDIBLE WILDLIFE ♡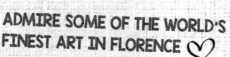

ADMIRE SOME OF THE WORLD'S
FINEST ART IN FLORENCE ♡

LOVE

GO BACKPACKING IN SOUTHEAST ♡

go on a truly
unforgettable
Road trip ♡

STAY OVERNIGHT IN A CASTLE ♡

SEE THE PYRAMIDS IN EGYPT ♡

VISIT DISNEYLAND ♡

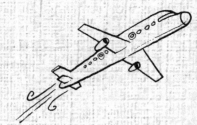

FLY FIRST CLASS ♡

THROW A COIN IN THE TREVI FOUNTAIN ♡

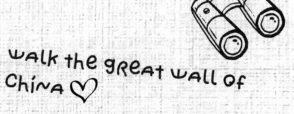

WALK THE GREAT WALL OF CHINA ♡

STAY IN A SUPER LUXURIOUS HOTEL ♡ *⋆Hotel*⋆

GO TO A TROPICAL PARADISE TOGETHER ♡

VISIT A SERIOUSLY CHEESY TOURIST
TRAP. LIKE THE WORLD'S LARGEST ♡
BALL OF TWINE IN KANSAS. USA

RIDE CAMELS ACROSS THE SAHARA (OR ANOTHER DESERT) ♡

EAT SUSHI IN JAPAN ♡

SOAK IN ICELAND'S BLUE LAGOON ♡

STAND IN AWE AT THE GRAND CANYON ♡

♡ 39

BE TOTALLY SENTIMENTAL AND KISS IN FRONT OF
THE EIFFEL TOWER ♡

Ride in a gondola in venice ♡

DRINK WHISKY, EAT HAGGIS, AND EXPLORE
THE HIGHLANDS IN SCOTLAND ♡

PARTY IN IBIZA ♡

TAKE A BOAT DOWN THE AMAZON RIVER ♡

CATCH A SUNSET IN SANTORINI ♡

VISIT AN ANCIENT CITY ♡

ACT LIKE TOTAL TOURISTS IN NEW YORK CITY ♡

VISIT RIO DURING CARNIVAL ♡

STAY IN AN ICE HOTEL ♡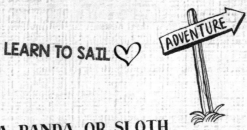

EXPLORE A RAINFOREST ♡

swing at "the end of the world" ♡

LEARN TO SAIL ♡

HUG A KOALA, PANDA, OR SLOTH ♡

EAT TAPAS IN BARCELONA ♡

♡ 41

FEED KANGAROOS TOGETHER IN AUSTRALIA ♡

STAY IN AN OVERWATER BUNGALOW ♡

go on a cruise ♡

HEAD TO MUNICH FOR OKTOBERFEST ♡

GO ON A SAFARI IN AFRICA ♡

TAKE A HELICOPTER RIDE ♡

 FLY IN A PRIVATE JET ♡

GO SCUBA DIVING ♡

GO DEEP-SEA FISHING ♡

BE ON A GAME SHOW TOGETHER ♡

ATTEND A SPORTS GAME TOGETHER ♡

go snorkeling ♡

CATCH THE SUNSET FROM THE TOP
OF A VOLCANO ♡

ESCAPE FROM AN ESCAPE ROOM ♡

CHARTER A YACHT ♡

SEE THE SUNRISE FROM THE TOP OF
A MOUNTAIN ♡

RUN A 5K, MARATHON, OR PARTICIPATE IN ANOTHER
PHYSICAL CHALLENGE TOGETHER ♡

DO SOMETHING CRAZY & SCARY – SKY-
DIVING, BUNGEE JUMPING, ETC ♡

ROCK OUT AT A MUSIC
FESTIVAL SIDE BY SIDE ♡

VISIT AN EPIC WATERFALL ♡

 RENT AN RV ♡

LEARN A NEW LANGUAGE TOGETHER ♡

ATTEND A MASSIVE NEW YEAR'S EVE
CELEBRATION ♡

EXPERIENCE A TOTAL ECLIPSE ♡

Ride horses along the Beach ♡

CLIMB A TALL MOUNTAIN ♡

STAY IN A TREE HOUSE ♡

DO SOMETHING COMPLETELY UNSELFISH
FOR THE OTHER PERSON ♡

SEE WHERE YOUR SWEETIE GREW UP: VISIT
ONE ANOTHER'S HOMETOWNS ♡

KISS IN THE RAIN ♡

LEARN TO DANCE ♡

FIND YOUR SPECIAL SONG. ♡

TAKE A COOKING CLASS TOGETHER ♡

find out how the other takes his coffee. ♡

RECREATE YOUR FIRST DATE ♡

CELEBRATE EVERY ANNIVERSARY ♡

have a ROMANTIC photo session ♡

♡
♡ WRITE LOVE POEMS TO ONE ANOTHER OR
LOVE LETTERS ♡

SET REAL RELATIONSHIP GOALS, AND
WORK TO ACHIEVE THEM ♡

LEARN ONE ANOTHER'S LOVE LANGUAGE ♡

 I ♥ YOU

PRACTICE GRATITUDE OFTEN ♡

SURPRISE EACH OTHER ♡

MEET EACH OTHER'S PARENTS ♡

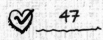

HELP ONE ANOTHER THROUGH A SICKNESS (NOT FUN, BUT EXTREMELY BONDING!) ♡

SHARE YOUR TRUE FEELINGS ♡

PLAN YOUR FUTURE ♡

KNOW ONE ANOTHER BETTER THAN ANYONE ELSE ♡

ADOPT A PET ♡

GET MARRIED ♡

HAVE A CHILD ♡

49

5 travel

Here you can set travel goals
for future journeys.

	Place	Date	Checkbox
1.	---------------------------	-----------------	☐
2.	---------------------------	-----------------	☐
3.	---------------------------	-----------------	☐
4.	---------------------------	-----------------	☐
5.	---------------------------	-----------------	☐
6.	---------------------------	-----------------	☐
7.	---------------------------	-----------------	☐
8.	---------------------------	-----------------	☐
9.	---------------------------	-----------------	☐
10.	---------------------------	-----------------	☐
11.	---------------------------	-----------------	☐
12.	---------------------------	-----------------	☐
13.	---------------------------	-----------------	☐
14.	---------------------------	-----------------	☐
15.	---------------------------	-----------------	☐
16.	---------------------------	-----------------	☐
17.	---------------------------	-----------------	☐
18.	---------------------------	-----------------	☐
19.	---------------------------	-----------------	☐
20.	---------------------------	-----------------	☐
21.	---------------------------	-----------------	☐
22.	---------------------------	-----------------	☐

23. ------------------------- ---------------- ☐
24. ------------------------- ---------------- ☐
25. ------------------------- ---------------- ☐
26. ------------------------- ---------------- ☐
27. ------------------------- ---------------- ☐
28. ------------------------- ---------------- ☐
29. ------------------------- ---------------- ☐
30. ------------------------- ---------------- ☐
31. ------------------------- ---------------- ☐
32. ------------------------- ---------------- ☐
33. ------------------------- ---------------- ☐
34. ------------------------- ---------------- ☐
35. ------------------------- ---------------- ☐
36. ------------------------- ---------------- ☐
37. ------------------------- ---------------- ☐
38. ------------------------- ---------------- ☐
39. ------------------------- ---------------- ☐
40. ------------------------- ---------------- ☐
41. ------------------------- ---------------- ☐
42. ------------------------- ---------------- ☐

43. ----------------------------------- ----------------------------------- □

44. ----------------------------------- ----------------------------------- □

45. ----------------------------------- ----------------------------------- □

46. ----------------------------------- ----------------------------------- □

47. ----------------------------------- ----------------------------------- □

48. ----------------------------------- ----------------------------------- □

49. ----------------------------------- ----------------------------------- □

50. ----------------------------------- ----------------------------------- □

travel •THE• world

53

6 adventure

this chapter is for things like:

swimming with dolphins
drinking vodka with penguins
sex in rainforest

Type of Activity	Where?	Target Date	Checkbox
1. ----------------	------------	------------	☐
2. ----------------	------------	------------	☐
3. ----------------	------------	------------	☐
4. ----------------	------------	------------	☐
5. ----------------	------------	------------	☐
6. ----------------	------------	------------	☐
7. ----------------	------------	------------	☐
8. ----------------	------------	------------	☐
9. ----------------	------------	------------	☐
10. ----------------	------------	------------	☐
11. ----------------	------------	------------	☐
12. ----------------	------------	------------	☐
13. ----------------	------------	------------	☐
14. ----------------	------------	------------	☐
15. ----------------	------------	------------	☐
16. ----------------	------------	------------	☐
17. ----------------	------------	------------	☐
18. ----------------	------------	------------	☐
19. ----------------	------------	------------	☐
20. ----------------	------------	------------	☐
21. ----------------	------------	------------	☐
22. ----------------	------------	------------	☐

23. ---------------- ------------ ----------- ☐

24. ---------------- ------------ ----------- ☐

25. ---------------- ------------ ----------- ☐

26. ---------------- ------------ ----------- ☐

27. ---------------- ------------ ----------- ☐

28. ---------------- ------------ ----------- ☐

29. ---------------- ------------ ----------- ☐

30. ---------------- ------------ ----------- ☐

31. ---------------- ------------ ----------- ☐

32. ---------------- ------------ ----------- ☐

33. ---------------- ------------ ----------- ☐

34. ---------------- ------------ ----------- ☐

35. ---------------- ------------ ----------- ☐

36. ---------------- ------------ ----------- ☐

37. ---------------- ------------ ----------- ☐

38. ---------------- ------------ ----------- ☐

39. ---------------- ------------ ----------- ☐

40. ---------------- ------------ ----------- ☐

41. ---------------- ------------ ----------- ☐

42. ---------------- ------------ ----------- ☐

43. _____   _____   _____ ☐

44. _____   _____   _____ ☐

45. _____   _____   _____ ☐

46. _____   _____   _____ ☐

47. _____   _____   _____ ☐

48. _____   _____   _____ ☐

49. _____   _____   _____ ☐

50. _____   _____   _____ ☐

7 memories

Time capsule for your memories
with photo slots

59

1. Where it was: _____

2. When: _____

3. The coolest memory: _____

_____

_____

Discussion....

1. What was your favorite part?

For HIM ------------------------------------

For HER ------------------------------------
----

2. What was you least favorite part?

For HIM ------------------------------------

For HER ------------------------------------
----

3. What you learned about yourself and your partner?

For HIM ------------------------------------

For HER ------------------------------------
----

4. What would you do different next time?

For HIM ------------------------------------

For HER ------------------------------------
----

5. What bucket list item are you looking forward to do next time?

For HIM ------------------------------------

For HER ------------------------------------

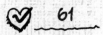

1. Where it was: _____

2. When: _____

3. The coolest memory: _____

_____

_____

Discussion....

1.   What was your favorite part?

For HIM _____
         _____

For HER _____
         _____

2.   What was you least favorite part?

For HIM _____
         _____

For HER _____
         _____

3.   What you learned about yourself and your partner?

For HIM _____
         _____

For HER _____
         _____

4.   What would you do different next time?

For HIM _____
         _____

For HER _____
         _____

5.   What bucket list item are you looking forward to do
next time?

For HIM _____
         _____

For HER _____
         _____

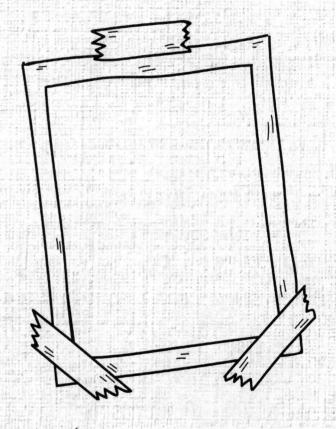

1. Where it was: _____

2. When: _____

3. The coolest memory: _____

_____

_____

Discussion....

1. What was your favorite part?

For HIM --

For HER --
        ----

2. What was you least favorite part?

For HIM --

For HER --
        ----

3. What you learned about yourself and your partner?

For HIM --

For HER --
        ----

4. What would you do different next time?

For HIM --

For HER --
        ----

5. What bucket list item are you looking forward to do
next time?

For HIM --

For HER --

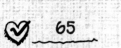

1. Where it was: _____

2. When: _____

3. The coolest memory: _____

_____

_____

Discussion....

1.   What was your favorite part?

For HIM
    _____
    _____

For HER
    _____
    _____

2.   What was you least favorite part?

For HIM
    _____
    _____

For HER
    _____
    _____

3.   What you learned about yourself and your partner?

For HIM
    _____
    _____

For HER
    _____
    _____

4.   What would you do different next time?

For HIM
    _____
    _____

For HER
    _____
    _____

5.   What bucket list item are you looking forward to do
next time?

For HIM
    _____
    _____

For HER
    _____
    _____

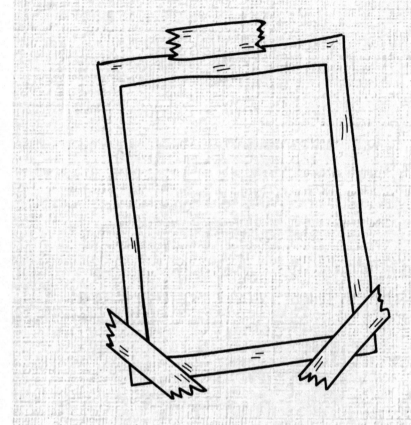

1. Where it was: _____

2. When: _____

3. The coolest memory: _____

_____

_____

Discussion....

1.   What was your favorite part?

For HIM _____
         _____

For HER _____
         _____

2.   What was you least favorite part?

For HIM _____
         _____

For HER _____
         _____

3.   What you learned about yourself and your partner?

For HIM _____
         _____

For HER _____
         _____

4.   What would you do different next time?

For HIM _____
         _____

For HER _____
         _____

5.   What bucket list item are you looking forward to do
next time?

For HIM _____
         _____

For HER _____
         _____

1. Where it was: _____

2. When: _____

3. The coolest memory: _____
   _____
   _____

Discussion....

1.   What was your favorite part?

For HIM
_____
_____

For HER
_____
_____

2.   What was you least favorite part?

For HIM
_____
_____

For HER
_____
_____

3.   What you learned about yourself and your partner?

For HIM
_____
_____

For HER
_____
_____

4.   What would you do different next time?

For HIM
_____
_____

For HER
_____
_____

5.   What bucket list item are you looking forward to do
next time?

For HIM
_____
_____

For HER
_____
_____

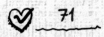

71

1. Where it was: _____

2. When: _____

3. The coolest memory: _____

_____

_____

Discussion....

1.   What was your favorite part?

For HIM _____
_____

For HER _____
_____

2.   What was you least favorite part?

For HIM _____
_____

For HER _____
_____

3.   What you learned about yourself and your partner?

For HIM _____
_____

For HER _____
_____

4.   What would you do different next time?

For HIM _____
_____

For HER _____
_____

5.   What bucket list item are you looking forward to do
next time?

For HIM _____
_____

For HER _____
_____

1. Where it was: _____

2. When: _____

3. The coolest memory: _____

_____

_____

Discussion....

1. What was your favorite part?

For HIM
_____
_____

For HER
_____
_____

2. What was you least favorite part?

For HIM
_____
_____

For HER
_____
_____

3. What you learned about yourself and your partner?

For HIM
_____
_____

For HER
_____
_____

4. What would you do different next time?

For HIM
_____
_____

For HER
_____
_____

5. What bucket list item are you looking forward to do
next time?

For HIM
_____
_____

For HER
_____
_____

1. Where it was: _____

2. When: _____

3. The coolest memory: _____

_____

_____

Discussion....

1.   What was your favorite part?

For HIM --

For HER --
----

2.   What was you least favorite part?

For HIM --

For HER --
----

3.   What you learned about yourself and your partner?

For HIM --

For HER --
----

4.   What would you do different next time?

For HIM --

For HER --
----

5.   What bucket list item are you looking forward to do
next time?

For HIM --

For HER --

1. Where it was: _____

2. When: _____

3. The coolest memory: _____

_____

_____

Discussion....

1.   What was your favorite part?

[For HIM]   ---

[For HER]   ------------------------- -----------------------
            ----

2.   What was you least favorite part?

[For HIM]   ---

[For HER]   --------------------- -----------------------------
            ----

3.   What you learned about yourself and your partner?

[For HIM]   ---

[For HER]   ----------------------- ---------------------------
            ----

4.   What would you do different next time?

[For HIM]   ---

[For HER]   -------------------- ------------------------------
            ----

5.   What bucket list item are you looking forward to do
next time?

[For HIM]   ---

[For HER]   ------------------ --------------------------------
            ----

Thank you for buying this book

If you like the book, please consider leaving a review, it will help author to create better books in the future

www.amazon.com/Nancy-Moore
www.amazon.co.uk/Nancy-Moore

Printed in Great Britain
by Amazon

35614450R00046